Norway

Deborah Kopka

🦎 Carolrhoda Books, Inc. / Minneapolis

Photo Acknowledgments

Photographs and artwork are used courtesy of: John Erste, pp. 1, 2–3, 12–13, 14–15, 21 (bottom), 32–33, 38, 40, 42–43; Royal Norwegian Consulate General, pp. 4, 14, 23, 30 (bottom), 32, 34, 37, 40, 41 (both); Laura Westlund, pp. 5, 21 (top), 45; © Blaine Harrington III, pp. 6 (top), 8, 10, 12, 16, 17 (right), 22, 24, 26 (top), 27, 28, 29 (top), 33 (bottom); © TRIP/J. Merryweather, p. 6 (bottom); © Kay Shaw, p. 7; © B & C Alexander, pp. 9, 11 (both), 13, 18, 19 (both), 29 (bottom), 30 (top), 31 (top), 35; © Ric Ergenbright Photography/Floyd Norgaard, p. 15; © TRIP/D. Saunders, pp. 17 (left), 31 (bottom); © TRIP/M. Jenkin, p. 20; Jetty St. John, p. 25; Peer Rødal Haugen, p. 26 (bottom); The Norwegian Information Service, p. 33 (top); © TRIP/GV Press, p. 36; © TRIP/R. Etter, p. 38; Steve Foley/Independent Picture Service, p. 39; The Nobel Foundation, p. 44. Cover photo of a mountain lake in Strynsvain, Norway, © TRIP/W. Jacobs.

Carolrhoda Books, Inc.
A division of Lerner Publishing Group
241 First Avenue North
Minneapolis, Minnesota 55401 U.S.A.

Website address: www.lernerbooks.com

Words in **bold type** are explained in a glossary that begins on page 44.

Library of Congress Cataloging-in-Publication Data

Kopka, Deborah L.
    Norway / by Deborah L. Kopka.
       p. cm. —(Globe-trotters club)
    Includes index.
    Summary: Examines the history, society, economy, and culture of Norway, about one-half of which is located north of the Arctic Circle.
    ISBN 1-57505-123-0 (lib. bdg. : alk. paper)
    1. Norway—Juvenile literature. [1. Norway.] I. Title. II. Series: Globe-trotters club (Series)
DL409.K67 2001
948.1—dc21

Manufactured in the United States of America
1 2 3 4 5 6 – JR – 06 05 04 03 02 01

Contents

Velkommen til
Norge!*

That means "Welcome to Norway" in Norwegian, the official language of Norway.

A bridge connects a small island to the Norwegian mainland.

 Imagine you're in a hot air balloon looking down at the country of Norway. It's long—1,110 miles long. But it's also narrow. Its width varies from 270 miles to only 4 miles. Some people say Norway's shape resembles a fish or a bumpy squash.

Norwegians call their country *Norge*, which means "the way to the North." It's easy to tell why! The northernmost country on the **continent** of Europe, Norway reaches up into the Arctic Circle. To the north are the Arctic Ocean and the Barents Sea. Also north of Norway is a chain of islands called the Svalbard. Norway's Jan Mayen Island and Bear Island lie in the Arctic Ocean.

Norway arches over the top of Finland to meet the northwest corner of the Russian Federation. The Kjølen Mountains form the northern part of Norway's border with Sweden, which sweeps along eastern Norway. Sweden and Norway share the Scandinavian Peninsula. The Norwegian Sea and the Atlantic Ocean lap at the western coast of Norway. Southward spreads the North Sea. An arm of the North Sea called the Skagerrak separates Norway and Denmark.

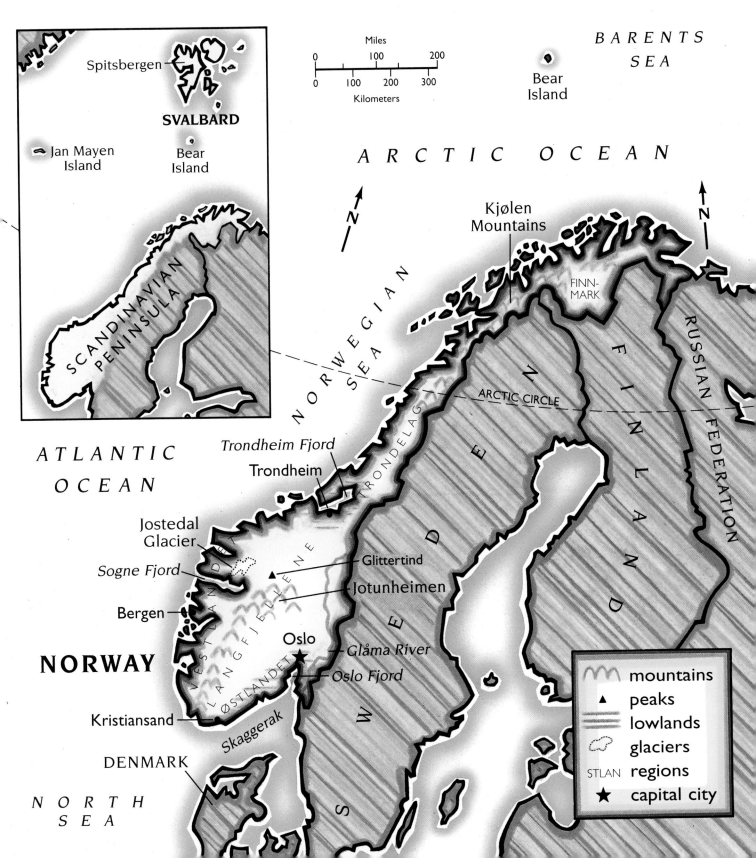

Spitsbergen

SVALBARD

Jan Mayen
Island

Bear
Island

Miles
0   100   200
0 100 200 300
Kilometers

*BARENTS
SEA*

Bear
Island

A R C T I C   O C E A N

Kjølen
Mountains

FINN-
MARK

N

RUSSIAN FEDERATION

SCANDINAVIAN
PENINSULA

N O R W E G I A N

S E A

TRØNDELAG

N

ARCTIC CIRCLE

E

F
I
N
L
A
N
D

A T L A N T I C

O C E A N

Trondheim Fjord

Trondheim

Jostedal
Glacier

Sogne Fjord

Bergen

D

Glittertind

Jotunheimen

V E S T L A N D E T

L A N G F J E L L E N E

NORWAY

Oslo

Glåma River

Oslo Fjord

Ø S T L A N D E T

E

W

S

Kristiansand

Skaggerak

DENMARK

N O R T H

S E A

	mountains
▲	peaks
≡	lowlands
⬭	glaciers
STLAN	regions
★	capital city

High in the
Mountains

A mountainous region called the Langfjellene runs from north to south across the southern half of Norway. Deep valleys separate mountains with forested slopes and snowy peaks. In some areas, the mountains are rocky and bare. Melting snow creates rivers that race downward to fill placid mountain lakes.

The craggy peaks of the Jotunheimen (above) **reach high into the sky. In the mountains are glaciers, such as Scartisen Glacier on Norway's western coast** (left).

The highest mountains in Europe north of the Alps are Norway's Jotunheimen, which means "realm of the giants." High in the mountains spread **glaciers,** or huge ice fields. On a plateau lies the 75-mile-long Jostedal Glacier. The plateau is snowy in the winter and covered with flowers in the summer.

The mountains slope into the sea in Vestlandet, or western Norway. Spectacular **fjords** wrinkle Vestlandet's coastline. The deep canyons lead from the sea into the countryside. Steep, rocky cliffs edge most fjords, but some wiggle through gentle valleys. Farmland spreads around Vestlandet's southernmost fjords. Islands dot the coastline. Some rocky islands called skerries only appear at low **tide.** Others are large enough for towns.

Facts about Fjords

Some fjords are just a few hundred yards wide. Large ships can navigate other fjords, such as the Sogne Fjord. The total length of Norway's coastline is 13,260 miles, including the fjords. Without the inlets, the coast measures about 1,110 miles long. That's the distance from New York City to Miami, Florida.

Heading **Downhill**

Farms cover the rolling hills near Oslo, Norway's capital.

In central Norway, the mountains slope near the Trondheim Fjord, creating the region known as Trøndelag. Mountains, valleys, and flat farmland make up the Trøndelag, where many Norwegians make their homes.

Most Norwegians live in Østlandet, the southeastern region of Norway. Here the mountainous **plateau** of the Langfjellene gently gives way to lakes and farming valleys. Forests thick with pine and spruce carpet the Østerdal, Norway's longest and

Fast Facts about Norway

Name: Kingdom of Norway
Area: 154,970 square miles
Main Landforms: Glåma
River, Jostedal Glacier,
Kjølen Mountains, Oslo
Fjord, Sogne Fjord,
Trondheim Fjord
Highest Point: Glittertind,
8,110 feet high
Lowest Point: Sea level
Animals: Reindeer, cod,
polar bears
Capital City: Oslo
Other Major Cities:
Trondheim, Kristiansand,
Bergen
Languages: Bokmål,
Nynorsk, Sami
Money Unit: Krone

A few houses lie tucked against a slope in south central Norway.

easternmost valley. The trees provide the wood for houses, buildings, and furniture. The logs are floated on the Glåma—the longest river in Norway—until the river ends in Oslo Fjord. Workers take the logs to sawmills in Oslo, the capital of Norway. With an area of about 175 square miles, Oslo seems huge to Norwegians. But much of that area includes the forests and lakes that the citizens love to visit.

Land of the
Midnight Sun

From May to September in Norway's extreme north, there is constant daylight. (This photo was taken at midnight!) But the sun doesn't rise between October and April.

The **Arctic Circle** cuts through Norway. This imaginary line marks off a circle around the **North Pole,** the world's northernmost point. Rugged mountains and craggy cliffs meet the sea in the part of Norway north of the Arctic Circle. Finnmark, or northernmost Norway, lies high in the Arctic Circle. Snow covers this high, flat, frosty plateau much of the year.

In Finnmark temperatures can plunge to -60 degrees in the winter. But summertime temperatures can

Electrical charges in the earth's upper atmosphere cause the spectacular northern lights.

soar to 86 degrees. The snow melts, but the ground stays frozen. The surface gets muddy and slushy.

Being so close to the North Pole also means that days and nights can last for months in Finnmark. From May to September, the sun always shines on Finnmark. That's why it's nicknamed the Land of the Midnight Sun. Between October and April, the only light comes from the aurora borealis, or northern lights. Even in Oslo, which sits in southern Norway, winter days are very short.

A full moon rises over a snowy Finnmark landscape.

Norwegians enjoy a sunny day in Oslo.

How's the
Weather?

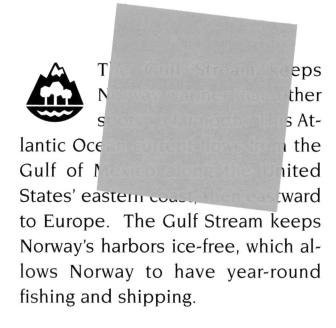

The Gulf Stream keeps Norway warmer than other spots so far north. It is Atlantic Ocean current flows from the Gulf of Mexico along the United States' eastern coast, then eastward to Europe. The Gulf Stream keeps Norway's harbors ice-free, which allows Norway to have year-round fishing and shipping.

The Gulf Stream and Atlantic Ocean winds give western, southern, and inland Norway a **temperate climate.** Daytime temperatures in the summer range between 60 and 72 degrees. For Norwegians, an 80-degree day would be a sizzler! And in the wintertime, temperatures in these parts of Norway don't go much below 15 degrees.

Wind carries lots of rain from the Atlantic Ocean to western Norway. Bergen, a city in western Norway, is the wettest place in Europe, with yearly rainfalls of as much as 80 inches! The mountain ranges block the rain from traveling to central Norway. It's colder east of the mountains, where heavy snows fall in the wintertime—but Norwegians don't mind. It gives them a chance to get out their skis!

A polar bear patrols the frozen Arctic Ocean near Spitsbergen, the largest island of the Svalbard.

A Long
History

The **ancestors** of modern-day Norwegians settled in Norway 10,000 years ago. They hunted reindeer and fished. Many historians think that the ancient Norwegians **migrated** from present-day Denmark and Sweden.

Norway's earliest people left stone carvings on these rocks in the southeastern part of the country.

Viking Longboats

Viking longboats were an important part of the Vikings' lives. The Vikings even buried their leaders in the ships! Sailors on the ships could travel inland rivers or open seas.

Craftspeople used the trunk of a single oak tree to make the keel (backbone) of the ship. Overlapping planks, reinforced with wooden ribs, created the ship's shell. One large square sail powered the longboat, but up to 30 pairs of oars let the Vikings row. The crew endured wind, rain, and stormy seas.

By 500 B.C. early Norwegians set up Norway's first farms. People made weapons, jewelry, and tools from bronze. By the Viking Age (A.D. 800 to 1066), Norwegians had become master sailors. The Vikings came mostly from southern and western Norway, as well as from Sweden. Vikings were skilled craftspeople, warriors, and traders who lived in **clans,** or family groups. They journeyed thousands of miles in their fast, long, wooden ships to colonize parts of England, northern Scotland, and Ireland. Viking clans also joined together to raid across Europe. The Viking Age ended in 1066, when the Norwegian king Harold Hardraade and his troops were defeated in a war with England.

From 1030 to 1380, Norway was a unified kingdom. Between 1380 and 1814, Norway was a part of Denmark, but in 1814 Norway united with Sweden. In 1905 Norway became an independent nation.

We Are **Norwegians**

When many people think of Norwegians, they imagine blue-eyed blonds, such as these brothers.

 Most Norwegians live in cities, such as Oslo. In each region of Norway, people are proud to have a separate cultural identity. Each region has its own **dialect**—a variety of the Norwegian language. Many Norwegians speak several dialects. Each area has its own *bunad* (national costume), which Norwegians may wear on special occasions and holidays. And each region even has its own traditional menus for special meals.

Despite these differences, Norwegians share many values. Most Norwegians love nature and enjoy outdoor activities. Hiking, climbing, and berry-picking are favorite ways to explore the countryside. Most Norwegians also share a common ethnic background.

Many are blond and have blue eyes, although visitors will also spot people with brown hair or brown eyes.

In recent years, people leaving their home countries to escape human rights abuses or to seek a better life have made new homes in Norway. Communities of people from Asia, Africa, and South America have settled in Norway's cities and towns.

This woman's bunad (above) **tells other Norwegians that she is from Telemark in southeastern Norway. A couple from Fagernes in south central Norway wear bunads for a traditional dance** (left).

Many Norwegians are proud of their Viking ancestors.

The **Sami**

About 30,000 members of the Sami (Lapp) ethnic group live in Norway. The ancestors of the modern-day Sami may have been Norway's first people. The Sami have their own language, culture, national dress, and government. Most of Norway's Sami live in Finnmark, their traditional homeland. Sami also live in Sweden and Finland.

Many Sami live in houses and work as farmers, loggers, or fishers. The children of Sami parents who choose a modern lifestyle live, dress, and go to school like other Norwegian children. But about 10 percent of the Sami follow their culture's ancient ways in the Land of the Midnight Sun. These Sami hunt and fish for survival. In winter they travel across the snowy landscape on sturdy sleds pulled by reindeer

A Sami girl wears her best clothes for a holiday.

or on speedy snowmobiles. They tend reindeer herds that live in the mountains in winter. The reindeer migrate to the coastlands in the summer. At night some Sami sleep in tents made of reindeer hide. A small number of Sami wear their culture's traditional clothes every day: a tunic (a long vest), breeches (short pants), and boots. Most Sami, however, only put on traditional clothing for special occasions.

This Sami reindeer herder holds a recently born calf.

Two Sami men cook a meal in their tent. A fire makes their shelter warm and cozy.

Fish is a common food in Norway, which has some of the world's richest fishing waters.

Let's
Eat

Big breakfasts are a favorite in most Norwegian homes. Kids eat cereal, cheese, cold meats, herring, and bread with butter and jam. At lunchtime office workers and schoolchildren pull out a tasty *smørbrød* or two brought from home. Smørbrøds are open-face sandwiches topped with pickled herring, smoked fish, lamb, shrimp, or salmon. Another favorite smørbrød topping is a brown, sweet goat cheese called *geitost.* Some folks compare its flavor to caramel.

Drop into a Norwegian home at *middag* (evening dinner), and you'll get a filling meal of meat, fish, potatoes, and dessert. Traditional dishes include *lefse* (potato pancakes), lamb and cabbage stew, meatballs with gravy, baked leg of mutton, and baked cod. For dessert you'll dig into sweet treats like a cream layer cake.

For special occasions, Norwegians entertain their guests with **buffet** meals called *koldtbord,* or cold table. At a koldtbord, people choose what they like from heaping platters of meat, seafood, cheeses, and wafer-thin bread. Even after a heavy dinner, Norwegians still have room for an evening snack. A late supper of smørbrøds may round out the day before bedtime!

Mind Your Manners!

If a Norwegian invites you home for dinner, never begin eating before your host does. When someone passes you a dish, take only the amount of food you know you can eat. Norwegians find it rude to leave food on the plate.

Bokmål or **Nynorsk?**

These fishermen might be speaking Bokmål or Nynorsk to each other.

Norway has two official versions of the Norwegian language. Bokmål developed from Danish between 1380 and 1814 (the years when Denmark ruled Norway). About 80 percent of Norwegians speak Bokmål every day. People created Nynorsk (new Norwegian) in the 1800s. Some felt

Norway needed a national language. People combined parts of Norwegian dialects to make Nynorsk. Bokmål and Nynorsk appear in books, magazines, and broadcasting.

Outside major cities, you'll hear many local Norwegian dialects. However, Norwegians can understand anyone who speaks and reads

The Norwegian alphabet has three more letters than English has: Æ, Ø, and Å.

Bokmål, Nynorsk, or a local dialect. But no Norwegian can understand Sami if he or she has not learned it.

Local governments decide whether schoolbooks, tests, and written materials are in Bokmål or Nynorsk.

Sami children can go to schools where teachers speak the Sami language. Children of immigrants attend schools in their native language and learn Norwegian as a second language.

A Norwegian woman finds plenty to read at her neighborhood newsstand.

Children wear the funny hats they made at their Oslo kindergarten.

Time for **School**

In mid-August, the Norwegian school year starts. Kids walk, ride a bike, or catch a bus to school. It might be an exciting trip! Many Norwegian roads wind through the mountains. Fjords interrupt some roads. Travelers take a ferry across the fjord to connect with the next road.

Norwegian children start first grade the year they turn seven. They attend six years of elementary school. Students follow it with three years of junior high. After junior high, teens head to high school. Many Norwegians attend college.

Students in grades one through six don't receive grades. But they

24

still have to study! Twice a year, their teachers send progress reports home. Teachers grade students in grades seven through nine twice a year. The kids take one final exam at the end of the year.

During grades four through six, students have classes in Norwegian, religion, math, English, social studies, and music. In grade seven, they can study another foreign language, such as German or French. All students learn about Sami history and culture. With all of this activity, the eight-week summer holiday arrives quickly! It lasts from mid-June to mid-August, when students begin another school year.

Meet Andrea

Andrea is ten years old. She lives in a town south of Oslo with her mother, father, and two brothers. She goes to elementary school. She spends time on her homework after school. But she still has plenty of time to play.

Growing Up **Norwegian**

Two Norwegian boys (right) **are ready for a big day. Perhaps they'll go camping with their scout troop** (below).

Many Norwegian parents work outside the home. They might head to offices, fishing boats, or stores. When no parent is at home, a *dogmamma* (day mother) looks after young children. A dogmamma is a friend or neighbor well known to the family.

Kids in first through third grade can stay after school for activities. Older students join sports teams, scout troops, youth clubs, dance groups, and orchestras. At home kids study, read, watch an hour or so of television, or listen to music. They might play at a nearby park.

Norwegian kids do household chores like cooking, washing dishes, cleaning, and feeding pets. They even help with the grocery shopping. Children who live on farms might tend farm animals. Some kids help their parents on fishing boats.

The coldest days don't keep Norwegian kids indoors! On a chilly afternoon, children might ski or build a snowman. Their snugly wrapped baby brother or sister could nap outside in a baby carriage.

All in the Family

Here are the Norwegian words for family members. Practice using these terms on your own family. See if they understand you!

grandfather	*bestefar*	(BEHS-tuh-fahr)
grandmother	*bestemor*	(BEHS-tuh-moor)
father	*far*	(FAHR)
mother	*mor*	(MOOR)
uncle	*onkel*	(OHNG-kuhl)
aunt	*tante*	(TUHN-tuh)
brother	*bror*	(BROOR)
sister	*søster*	(SOOHR-stuhr)

Buildings, Old and New

Cozy, brightly painted houses dot Norway's countryside. Visitors can spot homes tucked into the valleys and woods or overlooking the shores of lakes and fjords. Wood houses line some city streets. Families in the bigger cities might prefer to rent apartments in large buildings. Some apartment buildings are glass, brick, and steel. So are some newer Norwegian office buildings, shopping malls, and universities. But there aren't many skyscrapers or high-rises in Norway.

Norway's most famous kind of architecture has been around for a long time. Norwegians built stave churches in the Middle Ages. At one time, 500 to 600 stave churches stood in Norway. Only 29 remain in

This tall yellow house is just right for a Norwegian family.

modern times, but some of them are 1,000 years old. The small, simple buildings had a short **nave** (the main part of the church) and a narrow **chancel** (the part containing the altar and seats for the clergy). A self-supporting post, or stave, created each corner. Workers filled in the walls with wood paneling. A wood-shingled roof topped the structure. A small, round opening in the roof let in the only light. Wood carvers decorated the door frames and even the roofs with complex carvings of dragons, vines, and leaves.

Stave churches, like this one in Oslo (above), **are some of the oldest buildings in Norway. Newer buildings, like the ones in Longyearbyen on Spitsbergen** (left), **might hold offices, stores, or homes.**

29

Hit the
Slopes

Swoosh! That's a sound you'll hear as people expertly ski down Norway's mountainsides and along its valleys. Norwegian children are said to be "born with skis on their feet." Tots start skiing at age two or three. That's also when kids learn how to skate and sled.

Norwegians spend a lot of time outdoors in the summertime, too. Folks take rods and reels to fish in fjords, lakes, and mountain streams. They also navigate the islands off

Which way to the ski lift? Three boys enjoy a day of skiing (above). **Soccer is a favorite team sport for Norwegians of all ages** (right).

Whee! Kids like to shoot downhill on their sleds.

It's fun to pedal a bicyle over a bumpy mountain track.

Norway's coasts in sailboats, motorboats, and rowboats.

Berry-picking in the country's national forests is a favorite pastime. Hiking through beautiful forests is popular, too. In every season, many people head for the seaside or to mountain cabins for relaxing weekends and holidays.

The country's environment is important to many Norwegians, who want to preserve the country's beauty and keep Norway a safe place to live. About 20,000 children, ages 4 to 14, belong to the Inky Arms Environmental Detectives Club.

Inky Arms is an imaginary octopus who lives in the sea and feels the impact of humans on his environment. Club members work to find solutions to environmental problems like pollution.

Keep the
Beat!

From the classroom to the concert stage, music helps set the tempo of Norwegian life. Students join the school choir and learn a musical instrument, such as the violin, trumpet, or flute. Many perform in their school's brass band during the May 17 Constitution Day celebration.

Adults love to sing in choirs, play in bands, and join orchestras. Thousands of Norwegians have performed in the world's concert halls. Many groups, including the Bergen Philharmonic Orchestra and the Norwegian Opera, win international praise.

One-two-three, one-two-three! Plenty of Norwegians join a band or orchestra for the fun of it.

Children and adults alike enjoy jazz and rock music composed by Norwegians and foreigners. Turn on the radio to catch the songs of Norwegian pop groups, such as the Dum Dum Boys and CC Cowboys.

Edvard Grieg

Edvard Grieg (1843–1907) worked for years as a choirmaster, a conductor, a teacher, and a performer. Henrik Ibsen, a playwright, asked Grieg to compose music for his play *Peer Gynt*. Grieg used harmonies from Norwegian folk music to create what became one of the world's most famous pieces of music. In modern times, music lovers honor Grieg as one of the greatest composers of all time.

Folk music, which dates back to ancient Norway, is popular, too. People play traditional tunes on instruments such as the fiddle. Folk music influenced the Norwegian composer Edvard Grieg, who made Norwegian music world-famous.

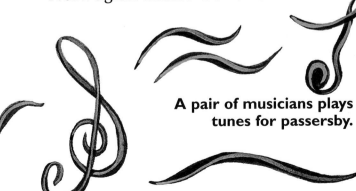

A pair of musicians plays tunes for passersby.

The Church
of Norway

The official church of Norway is the Lutheran church. About 90 percent of the population is Lutheran. Other Norwegians belong to other Christian churches. Few Norwegian Lutherans attend church every Sunday. But most observe traditional religious ceremonies. A Lutheran baby joins the Church of Norway through **baptism.** The service takes place in a local church with family and close

The Church of Norway is a state church, which means that the government pays clergy and takes care of church property.

... can belong to any religion they want.

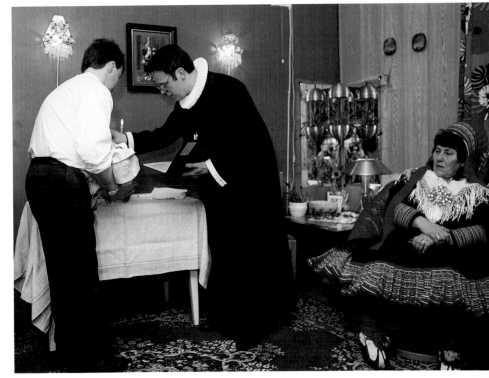

A clergyman blesses a Sami baby in a church service at the baby's home.

friends. The baby wears a long, white gown. After the service, guests gather in the baby's parents' home for a lunch party of traditional dishes and baked goods. The baby receives gifts, such as a first Bible.

At confirmation, young people declare their acceptance of the Church of Norway's beliefs. Boys and girls aged 14 or 15 prepare for Confirmation by studying with a pastor. During the Confirmation service, they wear a white gown over their "Sunday best" clothes or over their bunad. They pledge loyalty to the Church and receive a special blessing. Afterwards they gather with family and close friends for a celebration lunch, where the teens receive gifts.

Celebrating
Holidays

Make a bow and tie it tight! A boy and his mother wrap their family's Christmas presents.

On June 23, the longest day of the year, Norwegians celebrate Midsummer Night. People in each neighborhood light a huge bonfire and celebrate with singing, dancing, and feasting.

The year ends on an exciting note with Advent, the four weeks before Christmas. Families light a candle each Sunday. People make holiday crafts, such as fragrant clove balls. Some hang a star in the window to remind people that Christmas is near.

On December 24, the church bells beckon everyone to Christmas Eve service. Afterwards parents, grandparents, kids, and cousins gather for a delicious feast that might include cod, pork, reindeer, and turkey. Save room for mouth-watering cookies and treats, such as a traditional tower-shaped cake. A homemade gingerbread house decorates most dinner tables. Nearly every family serves a porridge called *rømmegraut* with an almond hidden in it. Whoever finds the almond gets a gift.

After dinner it's time to open gifts around the Christmas tree. Norway's Christmas season lasts well into January. But the excitement never dulls. Good food, good company, and good cheer fill each day.

Constitution Day

On May 17 each year, the country celebrates Constitution Day. On this date in 1814, Norway became independent of Denmark. Since the 1840s, this celebration has included a children's procession. In modern times, everyone has the day off. Thousands of children in every city and town dress in their bunads. The kids march through the streets, playing in school bands. Both children and adults enjoy sports, games, and magic shows.

These young Norwegians enjoy the parades on Constitution Day.

Wearing a bunad that she stitched, a woman displays a handmade basket and other wooden articles. The basket is painted in rose maaling, a traditional Norwegian style of decoration.

Made by
Hand

Folk art is decorative art made by people who aren't trained artists. In past times, Norwegian farmers created folk art to sell for extra money. Over time, many folk artists became skilled craftspeople hired to work in cities and towns.

Norway's forests give the country's wood carvers plenty of material. Farmers carve beautiful tables and chairs. Wood workers in the cities carve complex designs like flowers and angels on church altars and doors. Many Norwegians proudly use hand-carved utensils and furniture.

A style of painting called *rose maaling* became popular in the eighteenth century. Farmers painted their furniture, equipment, and utensils with colorful swirls of flowers, leaves, and birds. In modern-day Norway you'll see it on houses, churches, furniture, and household items. Each district in Norway has its own rose maaling style.

In addition to wood carving and rose maaling, other types of folk art abound in Norway. Many Norwegians take classes to learn ancient arts, such as weaving. Norwegian homes typically boast hand-woven rugs and table runners. People sew the family's bunads. Men and women knit warm winter woolens. Wearers treasure thick Norwegian sweaters with beautiful snowflake patterns.

Make a Clove Ball!

Norwegians make fragrant clove balls at Christmastime. The scent reminds them that the holiday is near! But you can make this craft at any time of year.

You will need:

1 large fresh navel orange
1 cup of whole cloves

1. Wash off the orange with a damp kitchen towel.
2. Allow the orange to sit at room temperature for one hour.
3. Gently push the cloves into the orange, one at a time. Work on one small area, than move to the next one until you have covered the entire orange.
4. Inhale the spicy scent, which will last long after the orange has dried!

Grab a
Book!

With the long, dark winters in Norway, it's no wonder Norwegians enjoy a relaxing indoor activity like reading. They love the current best-sellers. But they also love the literature of Norway's past.

Modern-day Norwegians enjoy plays written in the late 1800s and early 1900s, Norway's Golden Age of Literature. People all over the world know Norway's most famous playwright, Henrik Ibsen (1828–1906).

Bjørnstjerne Bjørnson (1832–1910) wrote stories, novels, poetry, and plays. He also wrote the words to the Norwegian national anthem.

Henrik Ibsen's 25 plays still entertain people all over the world.

The Norwegian author Knut Hamsun (below) won the world-famous Nobel Prize for literature in 1920.

Sigrid Undset (above) **won the award in 1928. Both writers' works have been translated into many languages.**

Author Knut Hamsun (1859–1952) wrote *The Growth of the Soil*. And Sigrid Undset (1882–1949) authored *Kristin Lavransdatter*, which tells the story of a girl in thirteenth-century Norway.

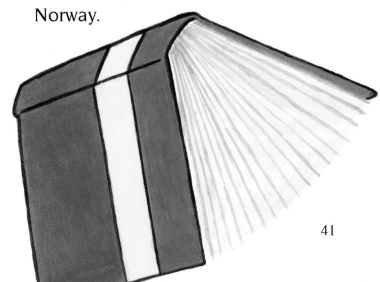

41

Once Upon
a Time . . .

That phrase begins many of Norway's folktales, stories that have passed from generation to generation. The ancient tales usually have happy endings, with good rewarded and evil punished. Norwegian folktales often tell of heroes who outsmart mythical giants and trolls. Trolls are creatures who make life miserable for people. They prowl around at night because sunlight turns them to stone. They create mischief then scurry back to their caves before dawn.

Three Billy Goats Gruff

Once upon a time, a small goat skipped over a bridge leading to a grassy meadow. But a troll living under the bridge wanted to eat the goat. The goat begged the troll to wait for the little goat's bigger brother. A bigger goat would be a better meal for the hungry troll! So the troll let the little goat pass to the grassy meadow.

When a medium-size goat came trotting across the bridge, it persuaded the troll to wait to eat his even bigger brother. The troll agreed to wait for his supper. Soon a huge goat with splendid horns came thundering across the bridge. The troll jumped onto the bridge, ready for his feast. But the large goat used his horns to toss the troll off the bridge, and he joined his brothers in the meadow.

Glossary

ancestor: A long-ago relative, such as a great-great-great grandparent.

Arctic Circle: The region around the North Pole.

baptism: A Christian ceremony that brings people into the religion by sprinkling them with water or by immersing them in water.

buffet: Platters of food on a table from which people fill their plates.

chancel: The part of a church that is around the altar.

clan: A group of families who have a common ancestor.

continent: One of the six or seven great divisions of land on the globe.

dialect: A regional variety of language that has different pronunciations from other regional varieties of the same language.

The Nobel Prize

Alfred Nobel (1833–1896) was the Swedish inventor of dynamite. He founded the Nobel Peace Prize. A person or institution who has done outstanding work promoting unity receives the prize. The Norwegian Storting (legislative group) picks a Nobel Committee to award the prize each year. People also win Nobel Prizes for literature and science.

Norway's Flag

Norway's flag looks a lot like Denmark's red flag with a white cross. In 1821 Norwegians added the blue stripe. In 1898 it became the official flag of Norway.

fjord: A narrow inlet from the ocean. Fjords are often bounded by steep cliffs.

glacier: A large mass of ice and snow.

migrate: To move from one region or country to another place. Some people migrate with the seasons.

nave: The main part of a church, where seats for parishioners are located.

North Pole: The northernmost point on the earth's surface.

plateau: A long, wide area of high land.

temperate climate: Year-round weather that is neither extremely hot nor extremely cold.

tide: The rise and fall of the level of the ocean that occurs every 12 hours.

Pronunciation Guide

aurora borealis	ah-ROH-rah boh-ree-AH-lihs
Bjørnstjerne Bjørnson	BYUHRNS-tyehr-neh BYUHRN-sohn
Bokmål	BOOK-mahwl
bunad	BOO-nahd
dogmamma	DAHG-mah-mah
Edvard Grieg	EHD-vahrd GRIHG
fjord	FYAHRD
geitost	GHEE-tohst
Glåma	GLAH-mah
Henrik Ibsen	HEHN-rihk IHP-sehn
Harold Hardraade	HAIR-ahwld HAHR-rahd-eh
Jostedal	YAHS-teh-dahl
Kjølen	SHUH-lehn
Knut Hamsun	NEWT HAHM-sewn
koldtbord	KOHLT-bewr
lefse	LEHF-suh
middag	mihd-dawg
Nynorsk	NEE-nohshk
Østerdal	UHS-tehr-dahl
Østlandet	UHS-lan-deht
rømmegraut	RUH-muhg-ruht
Sigrid Undset	ZIHG-rihd EWN-seht
Skaggerak	SKAH-geh-rahk
smørbrød	SMUHR-bruhr
Sogne	SEWNG-neh
Svalbard	SFAHL-bahr
Trondheim	TRAHN-heym
Vestlandet	VAYS-lahn-eht
Velkommen til Norge	vehl-KOHM-mehn TIL NAHR-geh

Further Reading

Charbonneau, Claudette, and Patricia Slade Lander. *The Land and People of Norway*. New York: HarperCollins Publishers, 1992.

Gascoyne, David. *Let's Visit Norway*. London: Burke Publishing Company Limited, 1984.

Haviland, Virginia. *Favorite Fairy Tales Told in Norway*. Boston: Little, Brown and Company, 1961.

Hintz, Martin. *Enchantment of the World: Norway*. Chicago: Children's Press, 1982.

James, Alan. *Lapps: Reindeer Herders of Lapland*. Vero Beach, FL: Rourke Publications, Inc., 1989.

Lye, Keith. *Take a Trip to Norway*. London: Franklin Watts, 1984.

Malam, John. *Thor Heyerdahl*. Minneapolis: Carolrhoda Books, 1999.

Norway in Pictures. Minneapolis: Lerner Publications Company, 1995.

Orton, Gavin. *Scandinavia*. London: Macdonald Educational Limited, 1979.

Pitkänen, Matti A. *Grandchildren of the Vikings*. Minneapolis: Carolrhoda Books, 1996.

St. John, Jetty. *A Family in Norway*. Minneapolis: Lerner Publications Company, 1988.

Metric Conversion Chart

WHEN YOU KNOW:	MULTIPLY BY:	TO FIND:
teaspoon	5.0	milliliters
tablespoon	15.0	milliliters
cup	0.24	liters
inches	2.54	centimeters
feet	0.3048	meters
miles	1.609	kilometers
square miles	2.59	square kilometers
degrees Fahrenheit	5/9 (after subtracting 32)	degrees Celsius

Index

Title 6

948.1   Kopka, Deborah L. 00-573
KOP
         Norway.

$22.60

DATE